# *Goodbye Scottie Road*

The Photography of Peter Leeson

The Bluecoat Press

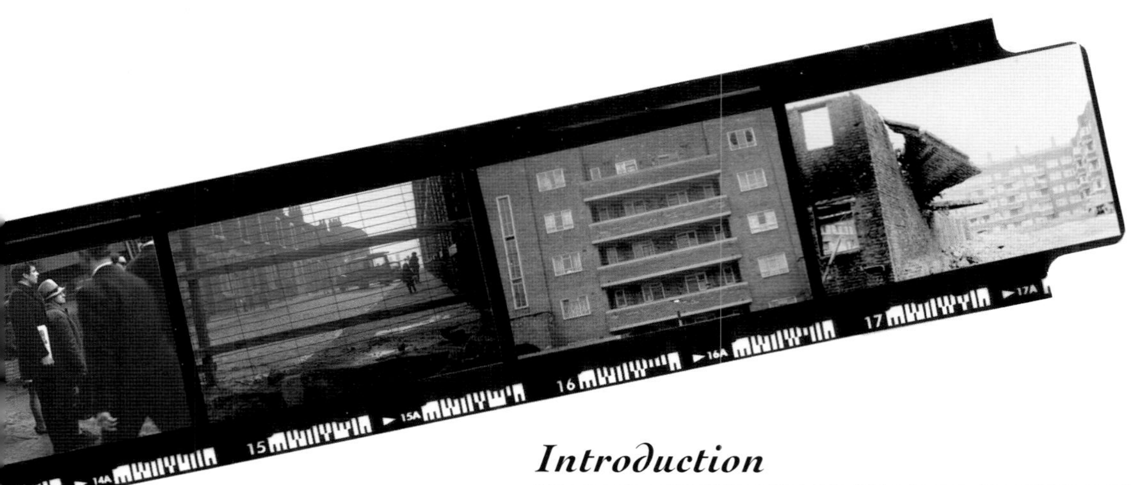

## *Introduction*

In creating the series, 'Photographers of Liverpool', I set out to highlight the value of photography in the context of local history. The saying, 'the camera never lies' is open to question today with digital imaging and manipulation but, historically, photography offers a unique window, freezing time and enabling us to see the past as though it was the present. By examining the work of different photographers, their individual contributions will be seen in the context of a history of photography of Liverpool which will map out the changing face of the city over the last 150 years.

Interestingly, although photography was invented in 1827, Liverpool, the nineteenth century boomtown, has a very poor surviving photographic record before 1880. This is not to say photographers were not active. The economic importance of the port guaranteed a dynamic culture but the sad reality is that only isolated images have survived and no single body of work from the first few decades has been discovered. This is surprising because ports with their mix of water, sail and dock life have always been an irresistible draw for photographers. Hopefully, sometime in the future, an overlooked collection depicting Liverpool in the 1850s and 60s will emerge to further our understanding of the city's dynamic growth.

As it stands, surviving collections begin in the mid-1870s and gather pace as technology rapidly extended the democratic use of the medium. The influence of Kodak, roll film and the first hand-held cameras meant that photography became more affordable and accessible to the wider population. By the early 1900s, it was estimated that there were over four million amateur photographers taking images of their families, streets and daily life. Candid photography had been born.

Over the course of the whole twentieth century, there have been quite a number of photographers who have documented aspects of Liverpool life, from those with purely commercial objectives to those whose intent was purely charitable. Others were driven to record a disappearing world, as streets and buildings were cleared to make way for the next wave of 'improvements', and some just interpreted the city for purely pictorial and aesthetic reasons. It is this contrasting mix of imagery that makes the compilation of 'Photographers of Liverpool' so exciting. The importance of photographers such as Peter Leeson cannot be overstated.

Peter Leeson started out on the side of the bureaucrats but soon realised that the residents of areas such as Vauxhall and Scotland Road had little or no voice in the decision-making that caused such a huge dislocation of their lives. Schemes such as high-rise flats and the building of the second Mersey Tunnel were pushed through without consultation in the name of progress. Faced by the destruction of the local community, Peter made a difficult choice and decided to leave his secure job and help give voice to the community. When the Vauxhall Community Development Project was set up by a Government initiative in 1969, he began to photograph the streets and buildings of the Scotland Road area.

*"A conventional photographic record of each and every street was not required. I needed to show the problems, but I also tried to show the life of the community ... Soon I was able to take up the challenge of writing and directing a film about the neighbourhood. Film-making was new to me but I was driven by a determination to "tell it as it was". I called the film 'Us and Them' to stress the contrast between the outlook of my new friends and acquaintances in the Scottie Road community and the remote decision-makers who had such a drastic effect on their lives."*

Peter Leeson's work belongs to the social documentary tradition which first emerged in Liverpool in the 1890s. Photographers including Frederick Inston, Thomas Burke and Lee Jones took to the new technology of hand-held cameras to create an invaluable record of people and places. Other photographers, usually keen amateurs, followed in their footsteps and the lives of the 'ordinary' people of the city began to be recorded. It is an essential tradition that needs people of vision, like Peter Leeson, to ensure there is a continuous record of Liverpool in all its aspects.

*Colin Wilkinson, 2008*

## *A Tale of Two Cities*

Back in the 1960s, I was a young designer and planner and, when an offer came along that would allow me to work in the prestigious Liverpool City Planning Department, I seized the opportunity. I remember coming to the job interview from Leeds, where I had been studying and staying in Liverpool overnight in a Mount Pleasant Hotel which blasted out wall-to-wall Radio Caroline.

In the January of 1966, my wife Gill and I came to live on Merseyside. The Beatles had long moved on but Liverpool still seemed full of hope. It was the Swinging Sixties and, to a young planner starting out on a new career, a future era of enlightened regeneration was beckoning. Or not, as I soon learned that the plans for major restructuring of the city centre were having a disastrous effect on Liverpool's historic fabric as well as being hopelessly out of touch with economic realities. The private sector, too, had lost the plot and the planners helped to prevent regeneration disasters. For example, a scheme was "discouraged" that would have replaced Albert Dock with a forest of office towers, the highest rising some 80 storeys. There was a 3D block model of the city centre in the planning office and when the scheme was included for testing, it was found that the winter shadows it cast would reach Lime Street!

Before this time, building conservation was not given high priority nationally. When London lost the Euston Arch, the public reaction helped to change these priorities. However, it was in Liverpool that the first Conservation Area in the country was declared in 1968, in Castle Street with its fine vista of the Town Hall. Even then, the planners had prevented a proposed high building from appearing behind the Town Hall, spoiling this view.

The old Cotton Exchange missed the boat and could not be saved despite the best efforts of the Council planners and the Royal Fine Arts Commission. Under the legislation that

*Left: Peter Leeson filming 'Us and Them'.*

then prevailed, developers simply had a right to replace it. However this does not explain later losses such as the Sailors' Home in Canning Place and the destruction of Georgian South Castle Street and Chapel Walks.

"Streets in the sky" were planned for the city centre. Although later abandoned, there are still a few reminders of this policy today. The major corporate buildings along Old Hall Street were to be accessed from a pedestrian plaza, two storeys up, with river views overlooking the notorious planned inner motorway. The entrances to these buildings are still at 2nd floor level, although the high level motorway was thankfully never built. Again, the entrance to the station on Moorfields is one floor above the street, originally to access another planned elevated walkway.

This explains why the lifts carry passengers from underground up to this level require an escalator to bring them down to the street pavement. Behind the offices, there was quite another city. In the 1960s, the poverty trap of our inner cities was not fully recognised or understood by officialdom. Indeed the official remedy of the age was slum clearance, although this led, in practice, to communities being pulled apart in a ham-fisted manner. Often families and pensioners were left behind for too long in unsafe, rubble-strewn streets lined with empty derelict buildings that once were homes to friends and family. The second Mersey road tunnel was being constructed but, to achieve this, it meant that Scotland Road, the heart of a renowned community was clumsily destroyed.

My father's family in London had already experienced the misery and destruction of such policies. In the 1950s, a much publicised study by Wilmott and Young had highlighted the effect of urban renewal on extended families in London's East End. Incredibly, in 1963, a former Chief Planning Officer of Newcastle, who later became Chief Planner at the Department of the Environment, could write:

*"In a huge city, it is a fairly common observation that the dwellers in a slum area are almost a separate race of people with different values, aspirations and ways of living. .. One result of slum clearance is that a considerable movement of people takes place over long distances with devastating effect on the social grouping built up over years. But, one might argue, this is a good thing when we are dealing with people who have no initiative or civic pride. The task is to break up such groupings even though the people seem to b e satisfied with their miserable environment and seem to enjoy an extrovert social life in their own locality."*

I began attending community meetings at a school in the inner city area of Holy Cross and was impressed by the dignity and common sense of the local people. I remember veteran, retired, Labour M.P. and national treasure, Bessie Braddock, honouring us all with her presence at one of these meetings. The League of Welldoers (Lee Jones) in Limekiln Lane was the venue for larger community meetings where Liverpool Corporation (the 'Corpy') officers did their best to explain policies to a disbelieving audience. The residents of Vauxhall had pride in their neighbourhood and there was always that special Liverpool humour. A transport boss met complaints that buses were regularly diverted to miss the area altogether with "If it says number 55 on the front of the bus then it's a number 55 covering the 55 route!" This was immediately countered by an elderly gentleman in the audience with "It says Cadbury's on the side but it's not a bar of chocolate!"

I carried a camera most of the time, attracted by the life of the City and the river light as well as by the architecture. As a part of my job with the City Council I became increasingly involved in photographing new buildings that were springing up - together with those that were being lost. A second-hand Pentacon 6 became a trusty, if heavy, travelling companion for many years to come. It looked like a giant 35mm SLR with a huge and sharp Zeiss lens and it produced 6 x 6cm square negatives. I set up a dark room in the loft and Gill and I developed and printed the black and white photos that are now part of this book.

When the Vauxhall Community Development Project was set up by a government initiative in 1969, I was asked to photograph the streets and buildings of the Scotland Road area and I gave up my secure City Council job to record the devastating changes that were inflicted by the road works and the clearances. A conventional photographic record of each and every street was not required. I needed to show the problems, but I also tried to show the life of the community.

Although the area was suffering hugely, today's residents, who were then children, often remember it as a time of freedom when they had the run of the streets and derelict spaces. There were bright kids everywhere, playing on the rubble-strewn pavements, in the derelict buildings and down the 'oller' or the 'debby' (as they called the left-over spaces that resembled bomb sites). I was noticed with my camera, but people were usually friendly and accepted that Scottie Road was a place worth photographing.

Later, Vauxhall Neighbourhood Council and the Eldonians were to rise from the ashes of the old Scottie Road, fired by a strong and enviable sense of community.

*Above: Still photographs from the 'Us and Them' film.*

## *Us and Them*

Soon I was able to take up the challenge of writing and directing a film about the neighbourhood. Film-making was new to me but I was driven by a determination to "tell it as it was".

I called the film *Us and Them* to stress the contrast between the outlook of my new friends and acquaintances in the Scottie Road community and the remote decision-makers who had such a drastic effect on their lives. I am grateful for the help of the CDP team, a crew made up of student film-makers, a sound specialist and an amateur film enthusiast, who are all credited on the film. Peter Maloney kindly read my script for the recorded commentary. I was fortunately able to include the views of Father O'Reilly, the local priest, whose local knowledge and pride in the area was self evident.

The residential clearance programmes were carried out with no regard for the human consequences. These Clearance areas often resembled bomb sites and rumour had it that sequences for the film Battle of Britain were shot around Scottie Road. Whichever direction the camera pointed, the same bleak truths were revealed. How could the authorities be allowed to treat local people in this contemptuous and off-hand way?

Traffic, too, was badly organised resulting in tragically high accident rates. Such disregard bred resentment and later led to organised community reaction. For example, city centre office workers always left a sea of cars parked around the streets and open spaces. This practice was eventually stopped quite suddenly when, after a long campaign, the community took matters into their own hands. One day, a group of mums whitewashed the cars with washable paint. They were arrested, but released in time to collect their children from school.

Although money was tight, children were always well cared for. I filmed a family of five excited kids having lunch and then suggested that we changed to a breakfast scene so that the sequences could be used to show their typical day. Afterwards I was careful to counter incorrect rumours that I had deliberately shown children being fed cornflakes for lunch! There was then a popular youth club including full gymnasium facilities and training at the 'League of Welldoers'. As I write this, nearly 40 years, later such facilities are not available in the area! With the demise of Scotland Road as a neighbourhood centre, Great Homer Street (often referred to as "Gratey") was the place to shop, albeit again across busy roads. Shopping was often wheeled in trolleys or prams along rubble-strewn pavements. In "Gratey", produce and prices reflected local tastes and pockets, with many small traders in tune with local needs. Capaldi's ice cream parlour was a favourite with youngsters. Historic "Paddy's" Market survives and bargains are still there to be snapped up but, sadly, the "walk-ups" - residential apartment blocks built between the wars - have now gone. Designed like castles, with modern facilities for working communities, the "walk ups" had communal access decks linking the flats and cementing friendships. Conversations often took place between decks. Asked to draw her home a young school child produced a drawing of friends holding hands beneath a sky of stars.

Violent Playground, a feature film of the fifties starring Stanley Baker, was shot in Gerard Gardens, the largest of the "walk-ups", misleadingly implanting it in the national psyche as a crime ridden urban ghetto. Paul Sudbury, who was born and lived in Gerard Gardens has chronicled the true heritage in his recent film Gardens of Stone. Short of cash for maintenance and modernisation, Liverpool City Council, as social landlord, allowed progressive deterioration until eventually the "walk-ups" fell victim to the clearances.

The *Us and Them* film needed weeks of editing at home using primitive equipment. When the film was finally delivered (expenses only), we were broke. However, I was lucky enough to find a job abroad. It would be a year before we returned to Merseyside. During that year, Gill and I travelled through Nepal, India and much of the Middle-East, always carrying my Pentacon 6. In Kuwait, I photographed Palestinian kids playing in the ruins of traditional Arab houses and streets as the old town centre neighbourhoods disappeared – a strangely familiar scene in a new setting! This was to be the overseas trip of a lifetime for Gill and myself, but it meant that we missed the community screening of *Us and Them*. It was many years later, when the film was "rediscovered" and became the subject of a BBC TV Inside Out broadcast that we were delighted to learn of its lasting value to the community. (The Vauxhall Neighbourhood Council went on to make their own film, which successfully opposed the Inner Motorway proposals). Recently, Vauxhall Neighbourhood Council used scarce funding to pay for the old 16mm master of *Us and Them* to be digitised and I have spent days on the computer producing a decent DVD copy.

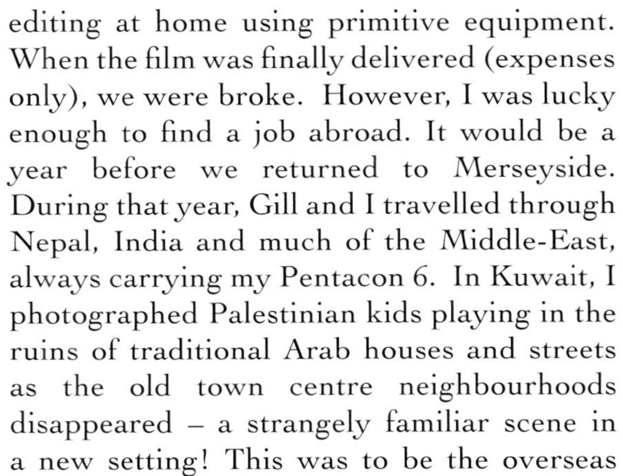

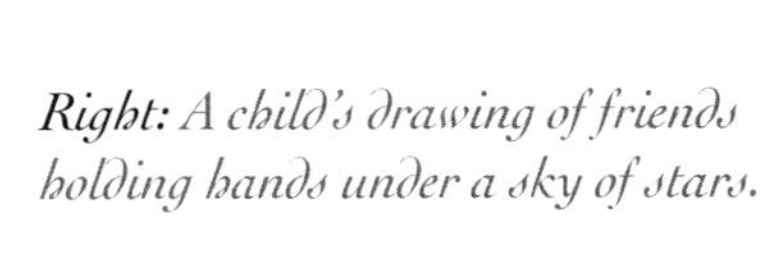

***Right:*** *A child's drawing of friends holding hands under a sky of stars.*

## *Dockland Action*

During my last years in Liverpool, I worked at Liverpool Polytechnic. Those years included the closure of Liverpool's South Docks from Pier Head to the Dingle and I became involved with a campaign to claim a stake for the communities in a redeveloped docklands. Also, the sudden worldwide awareness of the scarcity of fossil fuels, following the energy crises of the early seventies, had focused attention on the need to sustain resources. As today, green issues were at the fore. Here, we thought, was an opportunity to harness the enormous tidal range of the Mersey to power homes and development along the waterfront. We were helped in our work by a supporting address from the legendary Bill Shankly, whose speech stressed the need for jobs and training.

Again, the camera was used and I have many photographs taken along the whole two-mile stretch of dockland at a time when it had, like the Marie Celeste, quite suddenly become deserted. Being alone in the silence of that historic place on the edge of the land, where so much activity had taken place, was an eerie experience, but also one of life's unexpected privileges.

*Peter Leeson, 2008*

***Right:*** *South Castle Street from the Victoria Monument.*

MACSYMONS
SNACK BAR

CAPSTAN
CIGARETTES

*Left:* *The city centre at a time of change.* ***Right:*** *Office space to let.*

*Left:* *Fire at Lime Street during demolition to make way for the new St John's Market.*
*Right:* *Legal opinion.*

***Left:*** *The Piazza fountain, behind the Corn Exchange.* ***Right:*** *Charge of the light brigade.*

ST GEORGE'S HALL.
· NOTICES ·
TELEPHONE

SAMUEL
Britains
Largest
Jeweller
NEW HOUSES
SOUTH DOCKS
COME TO A MEETING
TONIGHT
7·30

***Left:*** *Street theatre, Church Street.*
***Right:*** *Lime Street Station buffet looked like a gentlemen's club (luncheon vouchers accepted).*

***Left:*** *Woodside Ferry. The tanker is empty, with the propellor half out of the water.* ***Right:*** *There were still three ferry services.*

I am
the
thy God...
thou shalt
have no
other gods
before me

*Left:* "*I am the Lord*".
*Right:* *Rush hour.*

*__Left:__ The Floating Landing Stage. __Right:__ Heading home 'over the water'.*

SMOKING SALOON

***Left:*** *This fellow traveller joined the ferry at Birkenhead and left at Pierhead. There was nobody with him but he seemed to know where he was going.* ***Right:*** *This was the Mersey, not the St Lawrence.*

*Left:* Arrival at Pier Head.
*Right:* Canning Half Tide.

***Left:** Gill. **Right:** Nicknamed "the dockers' cathedral", this grain silo was once the largest in the world. It was demolished in 1990.*

WAKENITZ

***Left:*** *Coburg Dock.* ***Right:*** *Cement silos, Albert Dock.*

*Left:* Scrap metal, South Docks.
*Right:* Fishing in the empty and deserted docks.

FIRE TELEPHONE
H
4 FT
JALAVIKRAM 15.4.6
פלמח

***Left:*** *Media exposure.*
***Right:*** *Rank and file against the Heath government wage freeze.*

FREE
MOTORS.

SMASH THE BILL
CAR MAKERS
KINGTONS

***Left:*** *Unions meet at Pierhead.*
***Right:*** *I managed to snatch this grainy action photo of Harold Wilson at St George's Hall the night before Labour lost the 1970 general election.*

***Left:*** *This aerial photograph from 1969 shows the true extent of the clearances that had taken place. Inter-war "walkup" apartment blocks such as Gerard and Fontenoy Gardens were reprieved for a time, until the next round.*
***Right:*** *A ground level view.*

Pedestrian
Route
SCOTLAND. ROAD.
CLOSED TO PEDESTRIANS
PLEASE USE
LIMEKILN.LANE/JUVENAL.ST.

*Left:* Local residents caged in by walkways. *Right:* Barbed wire.

*Left:* *St Anne's Street.*
*Right:* *Waiting for closing time.*

*Left:* Time to move. *Right:* One of the ladies in the foreground is wearing a traditional "Mary Ellen" shawl, while the younger generation in the background wear miniskirts.

*Left:* *Tate & Lyle.*
*Right:* *An urban playground.*

Mono Containers Limited
TAKE CARE DIVERSIONS AHEAD

*Left:* Driving practice.
*Right:* Recycling.

*Left:* *Football in Fontenoy Gardens.* ***Right:*** *Children playing in the 'garden'.*

*Left:* Fontenoy Gardens had a railway running underneath it.
*Right:* Between two blocks.

*Left:* *A questioning look.*
*Right:* *Refuge.*

*Left:* Refuge.
*Right:* Playing the spoons.

*Left:* Refuge. *Right:* The 'fish and chips' boat.

CHARLES WHITE L.POOL

*Left:* *Barrow boys.*
*Right:* *High society.*

*Left:* *Herculaneum Dock overlooked by the Dingle.*
*Right:* *Lifeline.*

O.F.R

*Left:* *A deserted Albert Dock.*
*Right:* *The Landing Stage.*

***Left:*** *Magnificent warehouses on New Quay.*
***Right:*** *Canal canyon.*

***Left:*** *Great Homer Street - the neighbourhood shopping centre.*
***Right:*** *An improvised playground.*

***Right:*** *This shopkeeper asked me to photograph her with her friend.*

***Left:*** *Herculaneum Dock, a dumping ground for concrete and waste.* ***Right:*** *Beyond repair (off Scotland Road).*

***Left:*** *Lessons not learnt, as houses off Princes Avenue are demolished, 2008.* ***Right:*** *Last resident.*

*Left:* *Woodstock Gardens.*
*Right:* *Defensible space.*

***Left:*** *Phoebe Anne Street and the Everton Water Tower.*
***Right:*** *Derelict flats near Athol Street.*

*Left:* Firewood. *Right:* "Look what they did to our street!"

***Left:*** *"It's not Hitler that's doing it."* ***Right:*** *Ticket to ride, a travel poster on Scotland Road.*

***Left:*** *"Take Children Out of Flats".*
***Right:*** *"Gardens and Flowers, not Heights and Towers, Concrete Mountains with Indoor Fountains, It's not Gift, Stuck in a Lift, When You're on the Early Shift."*

GARDENS
FLOWERS
NOT
HEIGHTS
TOWERS
LAND HOUSE
WEEK FOR
-INSECTS
CONCRETE
MOUNTAINS
INDOOR
FOUNTAINS
THE SKY
A57
PLAYER'S No10
TARTAN

EYES
STREET

***Left:*** *Eyes Street.* ***Right:*** *Corner shop on St Martin Street.*

***Left:*** *Great Homer Street.*
***Right:*** *Capaldi's ice cream shop was a favourite with children.*

PEPS
CAFÉ
Coca-Cola
refreshes you best
CAFÉ
Coca-Cola
LICENSED TO SELL TOBACCO
OPEN
MA

*Left, right:* Local shops and pubs disappeared along with the houses.

PENRHYN
STREET
INN
REBUILT
1889
FALLS

*Left:* Shopping. *Right:* Long live Paddy's Market!

Paddy's

***Left, right:*** *St Anthony's School, Scotland Road.*

***Left, right:*** *St Anthony's School Orchestra.*

***Left, right:*** *The kids made the streets their own, as the bleak clearance sites became their adventure playgrounds.*

LIVERPO
20 SOHO ST. LIVERPOOL 3
6/8 KINGLAKE ST. LIVERPOOL 7
TURNER'S AUCTIONEERS
ON TUESDAY, 7TH OCTOBER 1969
PLANT, MACHINERY,
STOCK & VEHICLES
ACTURERS

TOMMY
LIVERPOOL
BOOT.BOYS
G B
SKINHEAD.S
MIKE
IS ACE